My Mind on Jesus
Incarcerated, But I'm Free

Joseph Allen Ashe Sr.

My Mind on Jesus Incarcerated, But I'm Free

Poems By: Joseph Allen Ashe, Sr.

Editor: Anelda L. Attaway

Co-Editor: Rosalynn Boddy

Cover design by: Jazzy Kitty Publishing

Logo design by: Andre M. Saunders

Photography by: www.kairos2.com/helpinghand.jpg, Photobucket, ebay, Picsearch, Drimestime, deviantART by BenHeine, Godwin Whitehead, www.freejesuschristwallpapers.com, burningbush.jpg by Arnold Friberg, Gettyimages, photovision and Living Bulwalk

© 2015 Joseph Allen Ashe, Sr.

ISBN 978-0-9851453-1-6

Library of Congress Control Number: 2012908547

All rights reserved. This book is protected under the copyright laws of the United States of America. This book may not be copied or reprinted for commercial gain or profit. The use of short quotations or occasional page copying for personal or group study is permitted and encouraged. Permission will be granted upon request. Scripture quotations are taken from the King James Version, New King James Version of the Holy Bible. For Worldwide Distribution. Printed in the United States of America. Published by Jazzy Kitty Greetings Marketing & Publishing, LLC dba Jazzy Kitty Publishing utilizing Adobe and Microsoft Publishing Software.

ACKNOWLEDGMENTS

I would like to acknowledge God, who is my everything; without God, I am nothing. It is God who gave me the talent to write this book. It is God's spirit that moved through me in each and every poem. God's strength is perfect and it is God's grace and mercy that brought me through all of my situations.

Through God, I am able to be the author that I am today, and blessed to be able to present this book to all who choose to read, share, and enjoy it. It is God whom I give all of the credit, the praise, the honor, the glory, the thanks, and the recognition to for this book, and for every good thing that happens in my life.

Most of all, I would like to acknowledge and thank God for choosing me, using me, and moving through me to touch you. I just feel so blessed.

SPECIAL RECOGNITIONS

I would like to recognize the following below who have impacted my life in a powerful way. Each of them has left a lasting impression on my life!

To my aunt, Alice Riddick and my uncle, Joseph Riddick for their love, their help, their concerns, their chastisements, for trusting me, for believing in me, for pushing me, for holding my hand, for having my back, and for giving me a chance and being there for me when no one else would. You both have shown me love beyond all measure, and I thank you for being so great, so beautiful, and so special to me at an extremely crucial time in my life. Thank you!

To Agnes Owuso, you are truly a special woman. Even though all of your struggles outweighed mine, you still managed to be there for me, love me, trust in me, support me, believe in me, and pray for me. I love you Agnes, now and forever!

To Reverend Horsey of Alpha Christian Outreach Ministries, thank you for your time, help, teachings, and your inspiration. You were there for me, when I needed you the most. You have truly been a blessing to me, and I thank you. You are definitely a true and great Man of God.

To my favorite cousin, Reverend Doctor George W. Bratcher, Thank you for all of your love and support. You took me off of the street, when I was homeless. You also fed me, when I was hungry. You are truly one of God's soldiers, and I love you.

To Margaret Bratcher (Cousin Rainy), whom I call, "Mom". Mom, you took me in and tried to help get me straight. I call you Mom, because you have truly shown me a mother's love/concern, and you deserve the title. I thank you for all that you have done, all that you have been, and for all of your prayers. I love you, Mom.

To Anelda L. Attaway (JazzyKitty) who published my books. Jaz, you put this book together while I was in prison. I wrote the poems, but you did the rest, and you put it all together so beautifully. I want the world to know that I love you, I appreciate you, and that you are the best publisher that I could have chosen. May God continue to keep you, use you, and bless you.

To my sister, Rosalynn Boddy who is the author of the truly great book, "For the Sake of the Children," (Christy Ashe), which I encourage everyone to get and read. Roz, I love you, and I thank you for being such a great friend/best sister in the world to me.

To my son Joseph Allen Ashe, Jr. Joseph, you are my only son and I am so proud of you. Don't let life's struggles get you down, change your character, or cause you to make the wrong decisions. I love you son.

To my daughter, Jelisa Andréa Dixon. Jelisa, I am so proud of you. You are smart, dedicated and determined. You have always been special to me from the first day I laid eyes on you. I apologize that I was not a better father to you, but I am happy that we have a new beginning. I love you.

To my daughter, Tanesha Lanaé Dixon. May God's blessings always be upon you. I love you, "Little Bear".

To my brother Christopher Michael Ashe, Sr. Mike, I am sorry that I let you down and I didn't set a better example for you. I pray for your health/strength, and that you be blessed. I also pray that you won't make the same mistakes I have made and if you do, I pray that you turn your life around. I love you.

To my people who are in the struggle. To all of my people who are hungry, homeless, incarcerated, unemployed, broke, sick, and/or struggling with an addiction of some sort. I have been there, and I could never forget nor turn my back on you. My life will forever be spent serving God, and giving back to you.

This book is proof that we can overcome our circumstances. God is awesome, and He loves us. I pray blessings upon you all, and I love you. It is not meant for us to be down or stay down. God can help you, if you allow Him to. Please be encouraged, and let today be the day that you put your circumstances/life inside of God's hands. He will change everything. In fact, He has a mighty blessing waiting just for you, if you are ready/willing to receive it. I will keep you all in my prayers.

DEDICATIONS

This book is dedicated to my late-great parents. I miss you both so much, and I thank you for doing your best to raise a son like me. Even though, I made it way more difficult than you could have ever imagined, or dreamed. You gave me your everything, and today, I sincerely believe that you both would have been proud. I LOVE YOU BOTH!

In Loving Memory Of

REV. JOSEPH MCDONALD ASHE
MILDRED BERNICE CHRISTY ASHE

TABLE OF CONTENTS

INTRODUCTION	i
Dear God,	02
I Am Free	06
Hallelujah, Thank You, Jesus	09
I Thank You	12
Mirror	16
Think About It	19
Calling Jesus	22
Full of Joy	25
My God	29
Yesterday	32
Try Outs	35
God is Real	38
Come and Join	41
Be a Blessing	44
I'll Never Give Up	47
Sacrifice	50
Trust in Him	53
Don't Get Confused	56
Celebrate	59
Just for Me	62
Starting of Fresh	65

TABLE OF CONTENTS

Never Seen 68

Not by Myself.. 71

Save the People 74

My Mind on Jesus 77

Final Words 80

INTRODUCTION

God has chosen to use me once again, to bring forth powerful messages through poetry. Each poem was written as I was diligently seeking God's face. This book will truly bless anyone who dares to read and believe in the love, mercy, and the power of God. For those who don't know how to pray, this book will teach you. For those who want to talk to God but don't know how, this book will show you. For those who truly want to get closer to God, this book will help you. There are so many ways that anyone can be blessed, just by taking the time to read this book. God is truly working in my life today. Through reading this book, I pray and believe that God will work in your life as well.

DEAR GOD,

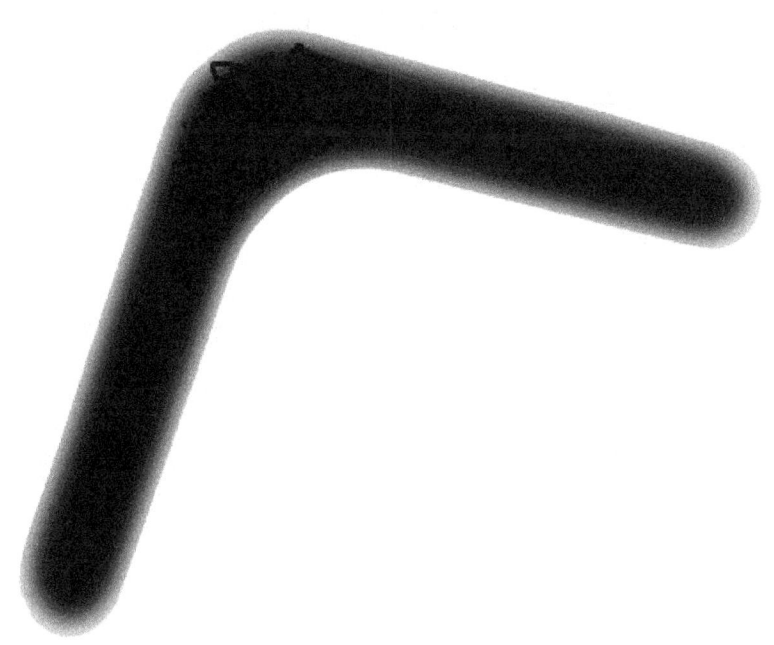

I THANK YOU FOR YOUR SON, BUT I'M SORRY THAT MY LIFE HAS EVER EVEN BEGUN. I WANT TO RUN, BUT I FEEL LIKE A BOOMERANG

EVERY TIME I TRY TO ESCAPE, I FIND MYSELF RIGHT BACK TO SQUARE ONE

Dear God,

If this is what my life was meant to be like, then I accept it. Yet, I believe that You have so much in store for me. I believe that You want me to do great things and to be a great person and have a much better life. Let me see what You see.

Reveal Yourself. Allow me to hear Your voice and see Your face in the midst of all of the trials, tribulations, and hardships that present themselves to me every single day.

Whatever I am doing wrong, whatever is holding me back, whatever You disapprove of, whatever I am lacking or slacking, "Please take it all away!" I'm on my knees right now Father. Please answer me when I pray.

See, my way has never worked and I am tired. I give up! I can't stand who I am or the things that I have done! When You look at me, what do You see? Who do You see? I thank You for Your Son, but I'm sorry that my life has ever even begun. I want to run, but I feel like a boomerang. Every time I try to escape, I find myself right back to square one.

I hear that Heaven is a MARVELOUS PLACE, but first You have work for me here on earth. What is my life even worth? So much suffering, so much hurt. I love my mother dearly, but sometimes I am angry that she even gave me birth.

This world is corrupt: murder, rape, drugs, homosexuality, liars, thieves, shootings, stabbings, kidnappings, child molestation, homelessness, diseases, disrespect, and destruction. Yet, You know what? I hear that Hell is even worse!

God, all I ever wanted to do was make a change and make a difference. Yet, look at how I am living. If You have ever planned to use me; what is my mission and what am I missing?

What? "Follow You?" You want me to go fishing? You want me to study Your word, obey Your commandments, give You praise, pray, and talk to Your people? God, You are real funny! Who will listen? Who will believe that I am a chosen one? Who will see Your light in me and follow? You want me to fast, give up bad habits, and seek You first. Wow, that's an awful lot to swallow!

What if I refuse? Oh, that's why I can't find peace and I can't find joy. This is what I've got to do. This is living right. I've been fighting the wrong fight. Instead of making a sacrifice, I've been beating myself up in life.

You are the Boss. You are the Creator. You are the One who knows and can do all things. You are the Alpha and Omega. You are the Beginning and the End. You are the Lord of Lords. You are the King of Kings.

You mean, I can have all that You have promised? If I do what You have asked me to do? The things that I've done can be forgiven and I can really become brand new? If I just believe and do then, all of this is true? **I thank You God! From this day on I promise, I'll follow You!**

I AM FREE

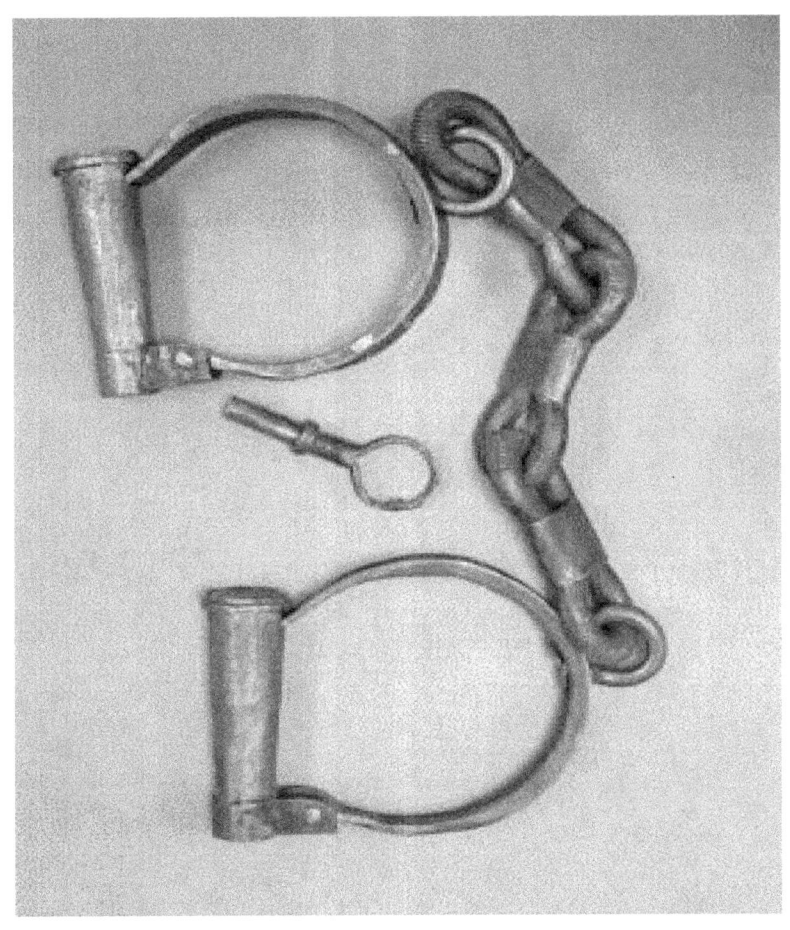

**GOD CAME THROUGH WITH THE MASTER KEY.
HE REMOVED THOSE SHACKLES FROM MY FEET
AND TODAY, I AM FREE!**

I AM FREE

Why am I even here?

In front of a bunch of people,

Who know NOTHING about me, At All

God gave me a Talent

And told me to Deliver a Message,

But is POETRY my Call?

Or was it Meant for me to Fail and to Fall

In Front of you all?

I BEG TO DIFFER!

Yes, it is True; I hold NO Championships or Titles

Except for the fact that I am Follower of Jesus,

Which makes me a Disciple

And when I Speak from my Bible

Some of you may get Frightful

Especially when I let my LIGHT Shine Bright
Exciting all who Hear me...
As God begins to Use me
And to move through me in this Poetic Recital

Yet, I did not come to Win
I did not come to Compete
And I Pray that in the End

I do not have to Shake the Dust off my Feet
But I come as a Living Witness
And to Testify to everyone that I Meet

When my life was Bound in Chains
And everybody thought that I was Beat
God came through with the Master Key
He removed those Shackles from my Feet
AND TODAY, "I AM FREE!"

HALLELUJAH! THANK YOU, JESUS

**YOU'VE BROUGHT ME THROUGH THE STORM
YOU'VE KEPT ME FROM ALL HARM
DURING THOSE TIMES THAT I NEEDED A HUG,
YOU WRAPPED ME IN YOUR ARMS**

HALLELUJAH! THANK YOU, JESUS

You've Brought me through the Storm
You've Kept me from All Harm
During those times that I needed a Hug
You Wrapped me in Your Arms

You Pulled me out of the Muck
You saw something in Me, that I DIDN'T See
My whole life I was Bound in Shackles
Until, You came and Made Me Free

So many times, in my life
I didn't say "Thanks"

So many times, that I Chose *not to* Pray
So many times, that I knew the Right Thing to Do
Yet, I Decided *not to* Obey

You NEVER Turned Your Back on me
No matter what, You Helped Me Through

There were even times I was Praising Myself
Yet, I FORGOT all about Praising You
Still, You were by my Side; Watching Over Me
Protecting me, every Step of the Way

I decided to Give In and give You my All
Now, I look at my life and I boldly say...
"HALLELUJAH! THANK YOU, JESUS!"

I THANK YOU

**I THANK YOU FOR THE GRASS
FOR THE BIRDS AND FOR THE TREES
I THANK YOU FOR ALL OF THE BLESSINGS
THAT YOU HAVE PROVIDED FOR ME**

I THANK YOU

I THANK YOU
for Waking me up this Morning

For Keeping Me Safe through the Night

I THANK YOU
For Opening my Eyes to See

Another day of Life

I THANK YOU
For the Air that I Breathe

I THANK YOU
For my Hearing

I THANK YOU
For the Food that I Eat

And for the Clothes that I'm Wearing

I THANK YOU

For giving me Shelter

I THANK YOU

For Heat when it's Cold Outside

I THANK YOU

For every one of my Limbs

I THANK YOU

For Tears to Cry

I THANK YOU

For the Grass

For the Birds and for the Trees

I THANK YOU

For all of the Blessings

That You Have Provided for me

I THANK YOU

For my Health

For my Voice and for my Brain

Without You Lord I have *nothing* so,

I THANK YOU, IN JESUS' NAME

MIRROR

**WHEN I LOOK INTO THE MIRROR, I'M CONVINCED
THAT GOD CAN DO ALL THINGS
HE TOOK A MAN THAT USED TO BE ON DRUGS
DELIVERED HIM AND GAVE HIM WINGS**

MIRROR

When I Look into the **Mirror** I see

A man that has truly been Blessed

A man that has come a Mighty Long Way

Because God's Hand is upon his Chest

When I Look into the **Mirror** I'm Convinced

That God can do All Things

He took a man that *used to be* on Drugs

Delivered him, and Gave him Wings

When I Look into the **Mirror** I see

A Glow that *wasn't* there Before

A man who has *never* been Worthy

Yet, each day, God Blesses him More

When I Look into the **Mirror** I see a Smile,

I just *can't* Wash Away

I'm Alive, Healthy, and Talking

When I *shouldn't have* made it through Yesterday

When I Look into the **Mirror** I'm Amazed

I LOVE EVERYTHING that I see

I'm *staring* at God's work and Admiring

HOW GOOD HE HAS BEEN TO ME

THINK ABOUT IT

DIAMONDS ARE SO PRECIOUS

WITH GOLD, THEY LOOK REAL GOOD

BLESSINGS FROM GOD ARE HIS PERSONAL GIFTS

THAT NEEDS TO BE UNDERSTOOD

THINK ABOUT IT

Roses are Red, Violets are Blue

The Grass outside is Green

It was meant for man to Live as Kings

For women to Live as Queens

Diamonds are so Precious

With Gold, they look *real* Good

Blessings from God are His Personal Gifts

That needs to be Understood

Forgiveness is a Powerful thing

Repentance should be done Daily

Prayer is our Chance to Talk to God

Yet, some of us Pray so Rarely

Deliverance is a BEAUTIFUL Gift

When God Delivers you, don't Turn Back

He'll Bless You Beyond All Measurement

But you MUST Stay on Track

Accepting Christ as your Lord and Savior
Is the GREATEST THING that anyone can do
The Gift of Eternal Life is PRICELESS
IT'S READY AND WAITING FOR YOU

CALLING JESUS

HELLO AND, HOW ARE YOU?
I'M HOPING THAT YOU'RE OKAY
I'M CALLING TO TALK TO JESUS
I NEED TO SPEAK TO HIM, RIGHT AWAY

CALLING JESUS

Hello and, how are you?
I'm Hoping that you're Okay
I'm Calling to Talk to Jesus
I need to Speak to Him, right away

I need to Hear His Voice
I need to Talk to Him, One on One
I need to Thank Him Personally
For EVERYTHING that He Has Done

I want to take my Time and Conversate
With my all-time favorite Friend
I want to go Deep and Apologize
For every last one of my Sins

I want to say, "Jesus, I love You!"
I want Him to Talk Back to me
I want to say, "Hi!" to God's One and Only Son
Whose Blood has made me Free

Can you please Pass Him the Phone?

Can you let Him know that it's me on the Line?

"JESUS I'M SORRY, I DIDN'T KNOW YOU WERE LISTENING ALL OF THIS TIME."

FULL OF JOY

TODAY, I AM PROUD TO SAY THAT I HAVE TURNED MY LIFE OVER TO YOU. MANY HAVE BEEN CALLED, BUT I PRAY THAT I AM ONE OF YOUR CHOSEN FEW. NOW ALL THAT IS LEFT FOR THIS WORLD OF CORRUPTION IS FOR IT TO BE DESTROYED. LIFE WAS MEANT TO BE SO SIMPLE AND "FULL OF JOY"

FULL OF JOY

Dear God,

When You created man, life was meant to be so simple, and **filled with joy**. Yet, the year is 2017 and to me, it seems like that dream has been destroyed.

I mean, look at this world today. Our children feel that it's okay to do and to say, whatever they want to do and say. Parents aren't setting a good example; there are so many children who don't even know how to pray. Yeah, they are so cute when they are smaller and all they do all day is play, but what about teaching them Your word, and Your way?

That has all been forgotten. You hear parents boasting about their children being spoiled rotten, and look at the news today. We have guns in schools, an 8-year-old girl gets shot, and the news ain't even shocking. I close my eyes and imagine her face, and tears just start dropping. But, I thank You, Lord, that it wasn't my kid in a coffin.

Drugs, money, and sex rule. Most young people don't go to church, bible study, or Sunday school. Nails done, hair done, tight clothes, make-up on, tattoos, and a hundred-dollar pair of shoes at 12 and 13 years old. That is far from Kool. That is why we have 26-year-old grandparents today, because we have parents that are fools.

Violence is not the key, and so many people are strung out on drugs. Suicides, overdoses, rapes, and murders; nobody knows how to love, and we are hurting. God, it is You that we should be serving; and as kids, we should have been learning. Now, we have diseases and infections with no cures. We are always at war. This world is about to end, that is for sure.

Yet honestly, I am not even scared. I am not trying to beware. Instead, I'm trying my best to be prepared. I have made my mistakes, but I have confessed my sins and changed my ways.

Today, I am proud to say that I have turned my life over to You. Many have been called, but I pray that I am one of Your chosen few. Now all that is left for this world of corruption is for it to be destroyed. **LIFE WAS MEANT TO BE SO SIMPLE AND...**

"FULL OF JOY"

MY GOD

**WE MUST TRUST IN GOD
GIVE HIM OUR ALL, LEAN ON HIS WORD
HAVE FAITH, FOR HE'S A MIGHTY GOD
THE GOD THAT WE SHOULD SERVE**

MY GOD

Nothing is Impossible for God
We must Give our All
Some of us may Slip sometimes
Some of us may Fall

God provides a way for us
To always get Back up
All of us go through things in Life
Yet, none of us have to get Stuck

Believe, Pray, Study, and Serve
Is what we all must Do
Praise His Name and Give Him Thanks
Never doubt, God's there for you

The Bible is Full of Promises
Each and Every one of them, He will Keep
He's a Shepherd in Love with His Entire Flock
And we're all His PRECIOUS Sheep

We must Trust in God
Give Him our All, Lean on His Word
Have Faith, for He's a Mighty God
THE GOD THAT WE SHOULD SERVE

YESTERDAY

GOD IS A FORGIVING GOD
AND OLD THINGS HAVE PASSED AWAY
IF I'VE LET YOU DOWN, I APOLOGIZE
BUT, I CAN NEVER TAKE BACK YESTERDAY

YESTERDAY

In my Lifetime, so many have Suffered
Somehow, because of me
I've used People, I've Lied, and I've Cheated
That's just how I used to be

I've Disappointed and I've let Down Everyone
That has ever been in my Life
Physically, Mentally, and Emotionally
My family has Paid a great Price

Those whom I Love, I have Hurt the Most
Yet, they all seem to still Love me
The Scams and the Schemes that I've Pulled Off
Is it enough if I just say, "I'm Sorry?"

Now that I am in Christ,
There is a Question that has me Stuck
Should I Spend the Rest of my Life
Attempting to Repay, Restore, or Make-up?

God is a Forgiving God

And Old Things Have Passed Away

If I've let you Down, I APOLOGIZE

BUT I CAN NEVER TAKE BACK YESTERDAY

TRY OUTS

KNOWLEDGE, WISDOM, AND UNDERSTANDING

DEAR GOD, THAT'S WHAT I NEED

PLEASE HELP ME TO CONCENTRATE

ON THE BIBLE

AND STAY FOCUSED, WHEN I READ

TRY OUTS

Knowledge, Wisdom, and Understanding
Dear God, that's what I Need
Please Help me to Concentrate on the Bible
And stay Focused, when I Read

Lord, I want to Live my Life
Inside of Your every Word
I want to be a Perfect Vessel so,
Through me, You can be Heard

God please give me the Strength and Desire
To Study, Obey, and Pray
Lord Bless Me with Your Gifts and the Power
To Step on the devil Today

Lord, allow me to Shout Your Name and
Give You Praise throughout the Land
Let me Sink myself inside of Christ
As if He were Quicksand

Lord place upon my Head a Glow

Like *no one* has *ever* Seen

Lord, I know there is a Spot that's Available

I JUST PRAY THAT I MAKE THE TEAM

GOD IS REAL

I'VE BEEN IN AND OUT OF JAIL
I'VE BEEN HOMELESS AND STRUNG OUT ON DRUGS
TODAY I'M LIVING PROOF
OF WHAT JESUS REALLY DOES

GOD IS REAL

I came into this World
A beautiful baby boy
To the **greatest Mother** who's ever Lived
I was her Bundle of Joy

I spent Thirteen years in School
I grew up Strong, I ate real Well
I learned how to Cook, Clean, and Dress myself
I've got a *million stories* to Tell

I've been In and Out of Jail
I've been Homeless and Strung out on Drugs
Today, I'm living Proof
Of what Jesus really does

I've been Laid up in the Hospital
I could have Died, I should have Died
I've only got *two* Eyes
But a *million* Tears, they've Cried

Today, I have a Home, I have my son,

And I'm Substance Free

For those who don't Believe in God

LOOK AT WHAT HE HAS DONE FOR ME

COME AND JOIN

I NEED TO SET AN EXAMPLE

I NEED TO STUDY HIS WORD AND OBEY

I NEED TO SERVE HIM FAITHFULLY

I NEED TO FAST AND PRAY

COME AND JOIN

Serving God has *never* been Easy

And the Task that I have is Great

I know that somewhere down the Line

I am going to make Mistakes

I just can't let that Stop me

If I Fall, I have to get Back up

God is waiting Patiently

In me, He has placed His Trust

I need to set an Example

I need to *study* His Word and Obey

I need to *serve* Him Faithfully

I need to Fast and Pray

God wants me to Recruit some Soldiers

He needs a Few Good Men

I'm going to tell everyone about His Army

Listen Strangers, Family, and Friends

He is Offering a *huge* Reward
For those who **Come and Join** Tonight
His Army is not about Hurting anyone
**IT'S ABOUT SERVING
OUR LORD, JESUS CHRIST**

BE A BLESSING

**GOD WILL ALWAYS BLESS YOU IF
YOU'RE WILLING TO BLESS ANOTHER
EVERY ONE OF US CAME FROM ADAM AND EVE
SO, WE ALL ARE SISTERS AND BROTHERS**

BE A BLESSING

Everything that God has Given to us

We must Give away

We are living Testimonies of the Mighty work

That God is Performing today

God has Done so much for us

And He wants us to Give It Back

Take everything that He's Done for us

And help Another, to get on Track

We all have Struggled sometime

Yet, God has Pulled Us Through

At one point, some of us had *lost* Everything

Now look, at what He's Done for you

God will Always Bless you if

You are Willing to Bless another

Every one of us came from Adam and Eve

So, we all are Sisters and Brothers

So, if and when you get on Top

Remember, "Your family needs."

Don't ever Turn your Back because

YOUR OWN BLESSINGS JUST MAY LEAVE

I'LL NEVER GIVE UP

MY LIFE IS NOT MY LIFE
I ACCEPT THAT WITH ALL OF MY HEART
I SURRENDER ALL TO MY LORD AND SAVIOR
I AM A WITNESS OF HOW GREAT THOU ART

I'LL NEVER GIVE UP

My Mind gets so Confused sometimes
Yet, I place my Trust in God
I know that He will Deliver me
He's my Protector, my Rock, and my Rod

I just want to do the Work of God
Yet, my Walk is Far from Perfect
I try real hard to be a great Vessel
And God Blesses me, but do I truly Deserve it?

I Love the Lord, He knows that I do
Yet, somehow, I still Fall short
Sometimes, I feel like Giving up
Instead, I Pray of course

My Life is not my Life
I Accept that with all of my Heart
I Surrender all to my Lord and Savior
I am a Witness of how great Thou art

God, I want You to know that

My Life in this Journey is extremely Rough

But after all that You've done for me

I'M NEVER TOO TIRED,

AND I'LL NEVER GIVE UP

SACRIFICE

**LORD, OPEN UP MORE DOORS FOR ME
THAT WILL HELP ME TO BE A BLESSING TO YOU
I WANT TO LIFT YOUR NAME ON HIGH
IN EVERYTHING THAT I DO**

SACRIFICE

Lord, Open up more Doors for me
That will Help me to be a Blessing to You
I want to Lift Your Name on High
In EVERYTHING that I do

You have Delivered me from all of my Mess
Now, it is Time for me to Fish for Others
Give me the Strength and Courage that it takes
To help to Rescue my Sisters and Brothers

Equip me Lord, with all that I need
I am Ready to Give my Life
I am now a Soldier in Your Army
Fully prepared to Die for Christ

There are people out there who are Dying
Lord, Use me; Let me be Bold and Brave
Place Your Glow upon me, Let it Shine Bright

Lord, let me Lead many to be Saved

Lord, I **Sacrifice** Myself Right Now

Take me, Mold me, and Use me too

**LORD, IF I DIE TODAY AT LEAST
I KNOW THAT I DIED SERVING YOU**

TRUST IN HIM

GOD WILL DIRECT YOUR FOOTSTEPS
HE WILL HEAR,
AND HE WILL ANSWER YOUR CALL
HAVE FAITH, YOUR BLESSING IS ON ITS WAY
YOU DON'T HAVE TO WORRY AT ALL

TRUST IN HIM

Praying to God is Powerful, In Fact
It's the Best Thing that anyone can do
He may not Answer *right away*
But, He *will* Answer you

It's *never* hard to **Trust in God**
Yet, being Patient is *always* a great Test
Our Prayers don't get Answered Fast Enough
But God's TIMING is Always Best

What can we Achieve by Worrying?
Does it make things happen any Faster?
What will Occur if we don't Wait on God?
Everything turns out to be a Disaster

God is Always There for us
He just Works at His Own Pace
Stand Firm, Believe, and Consider it done
Never Doubt, stay Humble, and Wait

God will Direct your Footsteps

He will Hear, and He will Answer your Call

Have Faith, your Blessing is ON ITS WAY

YOU DON'T HAVE TO WORRY AT ALL

DON'T GET CONFUSED

WHICH WAY DO I GO?
DO I TAKE CAUTION?

WHICH WAY DO I GO?

WHICH WAY DO I GO?

DO I TAKE IT SLOW?

STOP OR EXIT

WE NEVER HAVE TO BE CONFUSED OR
QUESTION WHICH WAY TO GO
WE JUST HAVE TO LEARN TO TALK TO GOD
HE'LL TELL US, AND THEN WE'LL KNOW

DON'T GET CONFUSED

Trying to do the Right Thing sometimes
Is the Hardest thing for us to Do
Satan tries to Twist our Thoughts
And He'll succeed, if we allow Him too

We *never* have to be Deceived
If we are Confused, we must Pray
Ask God to Direct and Lead Us Through
Trust Him, He'll SHOW US the Way

Satan is a Trickster who's
As Cunning as He can be
We must recognize Him, do not Give in
He'll Destroy you, and Destroy me

We must take our Time and be Careful
Trust God, He's got our Back
His word is the ONLY THING Powerful enough
To stop Satan, when He's on the Attack

We *never* have to be Confused or Question

Which way we should go

WE JUST HAVE TO LEARN TO TALK TO GOD

HE'LL TELL US, AND THEN WE'LL KNOW

CELEBRATE

SHOUT, "GLORY, GLORY, GLORY!"
STOMP YOUR FEET AND CLAP YOUR HANDS
SHOUT, "HALLELUJAH!"
FOR IT'S THE HIGHEST PRAISE
SO, LET US DO THE HALLELUJAH DANCE

CELEBRATE

When we Get up in the Morning
Let us all Stand to our Feet
Say, "Thank You, Thank You, Thank You Lord,
For all that You've done for me!"

Shout, "Glory, Glory, Glory!"
Stomp your Feet and Clap your Hands
Shout "Hallelujah!" for it's the HIGHEST PRAISE!
So, let us do the Hallelujah Dance

If God has been as Good to you
As He has been to me
Let's **Celebrate** the Blood of Jesus
The Blood that Made Us All Free

We don't need any kind of Beat
Let the Holy Ghost have His way
Jump Up and Down, give God the Praise
He Woke us up Today

Continue to Praise and Praise, all day

Because this is what God Desires

Give God what He deserves in the Morning

Then all Day, Just stay on Fire

JUST FOR ME

COULD I HAVE TAKEN THE PAIN?
THE SHARP THORNS STICKING INTO MY HEAD
AS I WAS BEING FORCED TO WEAR THIS CROWN
AND HEARING THE KING OF THE JEWS
BEING SAID?

JUST FOR ME

I can't even Imagine attempting to Endure
The Pain that You Suffered for me
I can only go by the Stories that I've been Told
Because I wasn't there to see

Could I have Taken the Torment?
Feeling the Whip as it Cracked Open my Skin?
Thirty-nine times, Tearing into my Flesh
Just Ripping, Again and Again?

Could I have Taken the Pain?
The Sharp Thorns sticking into my Head
As I was being forced to Wear this Crown
And hearing **The King of the Jews** being said?

Could I have Carried my own Cross?
Stakes Nailed into my Feet, Hands, and Sides
After all this, would I Love my people so much
That I'd come Back, three days after I Died?

I'll never know how You took it all
Yet, if I had NO EYES, I still Could see
That everything that You went through
YOU WENT THROUGH IT, JUST FOR ME

STARTING OFF FRESH

LORD, YOU BEGAN TO BLESS ME

I PRAYED, AND I THANKED YOU EACH DAY

SOMETIMES I EVEN HAD TO PRAY TWICE

BECAUSE OF THINGS I FORGOT,

THAT I MEANT TO SAY

STARTING OFF FRESH

Lord, when I first Surrendered to You
Everything about me Changed
The way I Talked, my Ways of Thinking
Were Far from being the Same

There were things that I used to do
That all of a Sudden, I had no Desire for
So many things I was Struggling with,
Then all of a Sudden, I Struggled no more

Lord, You began to Bless me
I Prayed, and I Thanked You each day
Sometimes I even had to Pray twice
Because of things I Forgot, that I meant to Say

Lord today, I Feel like I am Slipping
Like something I'm Doing, must not be Right
I feel like I am Struggling all over again
I Surrendered ONCE; Lord, I Surrender TWICE

Lord, I'm Throwing my Hands in the Air again;

You know ALL

Take this Weight Off of my Chest

I know that if I just keep Surrendering to You

YOU'LL DELIVER ME

AND KEEP ME STARTING OFF FRESH

NEVER SEEN

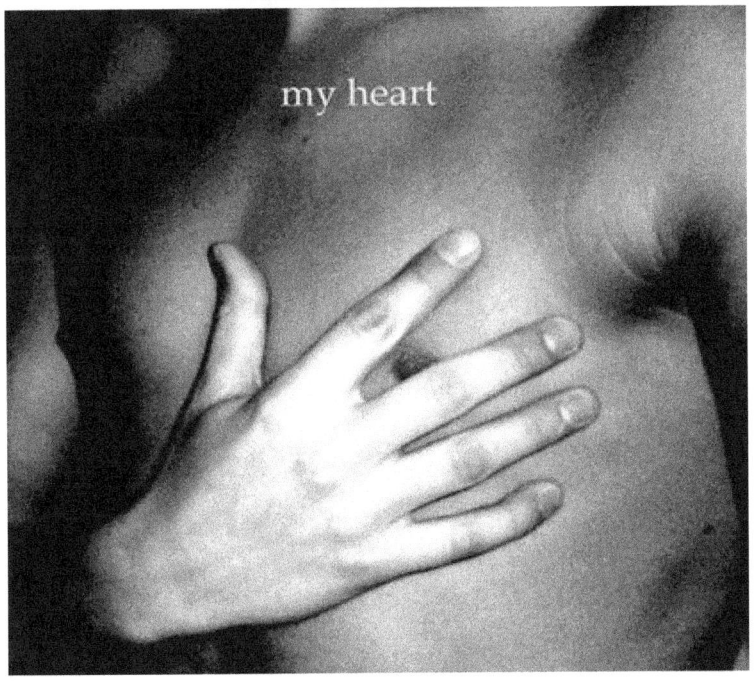

TODAY, I JUST WANT TO TAKE MY TIME
I'VE GOT SOMETHING THAT'S ON MY HEART
THERE IS A MAN WHO'S BEEN SO GOOD TO ME
I'M NOT SURE WHERE I SHOULD START

NEVER SEEN

Today, I just want to Take my Time
I've got something that's on my Heart
There is a Man who's been so Good to me
I'm not Sure where I should Start

I'm in Love with this Man, a Mighty Man
And I know this Man Loves me
One day He made a Tremendous Sacrifice
For me, on Calvary

I've **never seen** this Man,
Yet, I talk to Him everyday
He fills my Heart with so much Joy
And He makes sure that I'm okay

He and I are Together all of the time
He Holds my Hand; He makes me feel Warm
When I feel Weak, He becomes my Shield
And He Protects me from all Harm

When I'm asleep, He Wraps me in His Arms

He shows me Love, and He's never mean

His name is Jesus the Christ and He's

THE GREATEST MAN

THAT I'VE NEVER SEEN

NOT BY MYSELF

WHEN I DON'T KNOW WHAT TO DO
WHEN I COULD SURELY USE A HELPING HAND
WHEN THERE'S NO ONE THAT I CAN TURN TO

NOT BY MYSELF

In times when I've got some trouble
When I don't know what to do
When I could surely use a helping hand
When there's no one that I can turn to

When my situation seems hopeless
When a solution cannot be found
When I've paced, until I can't pace no more
When everyone else has let me down

When I've tried, but haven't come near success
When things become too much for me to bear
When I feel that there is nowhere else to look
When I'm sure that I've looked everywhere

When I've given everything that I've got
When my problems just won't go away
That's usually the time when I remember
That I forgot to pray

Jesus is the Answer to all things

In my time of need, He will help

Each time I forget, I will go through things

THAT CAN'T BE HANDLED BY MYSELF

SAVE THE PEOPLE

PRAY AND FAST

FAST AND PRAY

STUDY AND MEDITATE IN GOD'S WORD

BECOME THAT VESSEL THAT GOD CAN USE

TO MAKE SURE THAT HIS MESSAGE IS HEARD

SAVE THE PEOPLE

Attention all ye people
Listen Close to what I say
Jesus Christ is Coming Again Soon
There is NO TIME to Play

Men, you need to Grab your Families
Come Aboard the Jesus Ark
Just Believe and Confess that He is Lord
And Repent, with all of your Heart

We must Go out and Grab some others
Once we're Sure that we are Saved
Tell all about the Gift of God
Speak Boldly, have no Fear, and be Brave

Pray and Fast, Fast and Pray
Study and Meditate in God's Word
Become that Vessel that God can use
To make Sure that His Message is Heard

Before you can Say that you Love God

You must Love everyone, as yourself

This means, if you're Sure that you are Saved

YOUR MISSION IS TO

RESCUE SOMEONE ELSE

MY MIND ON JESUS

I FEEL A FIRE INSIDE OF ME
THAT WAS NEVER THERE BEFORE
I AM DANCING AND I AM JUMPING AROUND
AS SWEAT BEGINS TO POUR

MY MIND ON JESUS

I feel His Presence and His Peace

My Mind is totally at Rest

All of my Tremendously Heavy Burdens

Are Fleeing from my Chest

I feel so much Joy taking Over

In fact, I feel a Praise Coming On

"Hallelujah! Thank You Jesus!"

Are the Words that I Scream...

Until I can Scream no more

And my Voice is Gone

I feel a Fire inside of me

That was *never* there Before

I am Dancing and I am Jumping around

As Sweat begins to Pour

I feel His Power,

His Strength, and His Comfort

Building up Inside of me

Every Chain and Shackle that has ever had me Bound

Are Loosed and Now I'm Free

Nothing else seems to even matter

No Concerns or Worries tonight

I HAVE MY MIND ON JESUS CHRIST

AND EVERYTHING IS FEELING SO RIGHT

FINAL WORDS

I REALIZE THAT MY LIFE IS NOT MY OWN
I AM AT PEACE;
JUST LET YOUR WILL BE DONE

THANKS FOR CHOOSING ME
AS YOUR VESSEL IN WAR
THE VICTORY IS YOURS,
THE BATTLE HAS BEEN WON

FINAL WORDS

If my Time on this earth is Done
I just Hope and Pray that You know
I have Tried as hard as I could to Serve You
I Love You, my Lord; I'm ready to Go

I realize that my Life is not my Own
I am at Peace; just let Your will be Done
Thanks for Choosing me as Your Vessel in War
The Victory is Yours, the Battle has been Won

I ask You to Watch over my children
Let my Life be an Example for them to Live
Give them the Courage to be better Disciples
And to Win more Souls for You, than I ever Did

Lord, since I made my Surrender to You
I've been Your Soldier the Best way I know how
I'm Tired, I'm Weak, and I Understand
Thanks for Blessing and Keeping Me Until Now

Dear God, I am far from Afraid
It's about You, and *not* about me
If my time has come to Leave this earth
**I KNOW YOUR MANSION
IS THE NEXT PLACE I'LL BE**

www.ingramcontent.com/pod-product-compliance
Lightning Source LLC
Chambersburg PA
CBHW071834290426
44109CB00017B/1825